The Montgomery Bus Boycott

Kerri O'Hern
AR B.L.: 4.8
Points: 0.5   MG

GRAPHIC HISTORIES

THE MONTGOMERY BUS BOYCOTT

STORY:
KERRI O'HERN AND FRANK WALSH

ILLUSTRATIONS:
D. MCHARGUE

WORLD ALMANAC® LIBRARY

During the 1950s in parts of the United States, black people did not have the same freedoms as white people. In some states, African Americans could be put in jail for arguing with a white person. Black people could not eat with white people. They could not drink from the same water fountain. In Montgomery, Alabama, the public bus system had rules about where African Americans could sit.

ON DECEMBER 1, 1955, A BLACK WOMAN NAMED ROSA PARKS WAS ARRESTED IN MONTGOMERY. SHE HAD REFUSED TO GIVE UP HER BUS SEAT TO A WHITE PERSON.

AS A PROTEST, BLACK PEOPLE REFUSED TO RIDE THE BUSES IN MONTGOMERY FOR AN ENTIRE YEAR! THE MONTGOMERY BUS BOYCOTT THEN SPARKED ABOUT 10 YEARS OF CIVIL RIGHTS PROTESTS. CIVIL RIGHTS ARE THE BASIC FREEDOMS THAT BLACK PEOPLE WANTED. BLACK PEOPLE WANTED THE SAME OPPORTUNITIES THAT OTHER AMERICANS HAD.

THE UNITED STATES DECLARED ITS INDEPENDENCE FROM GREAT BRITAIN IN 1776. AT THAT TIME, SLAVERY WAS LEGAL. AS THE AUTHOR OF THE DECLARATION OF INDEPENDENCE, THOMAS JEFFERSON WROTE THAT "ALL MEN ARE CREATED EQUAL." BUT EVEN HE KEPT SLAVES.

WITHOUT SLAVES, THE LARGE PLANTATIONS WOULD NOT HAVE ANY UNPAID WORKERS.

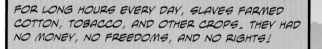

FOR LONG HOURS EVERY DAY, SLAVES FARMED COTTON, TOBACCO, AND OTHER CROPS. THEY HAD NO MONEY, NO FREEDOMS, AND NO RIGHTS!

WORK FASTER!

I'M SO TIRED AND THRISTY

BY THE EARLY 1800S, SLAVERY NO LONGER EXISTED IN MOST OF THE NORTH. THE NORTHERN STATES SPOKE OUT AGAINST SLAVERY.

SLAVERY IS HORRIBLE!

BETWEEN 1861 AND 1865, THE NORTH AND SOUTH FOUGHT A LONG AND TERRIBLE WAR OVER SLAVERY. THE WAR DIVIDED THE UNION.

IN 1863, PRESIDENT ABRAHAM LINCOLN ISSUED A STATEMENT THAT FREED THE SLAVES IN THE SOUTH. SADLY, IT HAD LITTLE EFFECT IN THE SOUTH.

SLAVERY DID NOT BECOME ILLEGAL THROUGHOUT THE NATION UNTIL 1865. THAT YEAR THE NORTH WON THE CIVIL WAR, AND THE UNION BECAME WHOLE AGAIN.

BY LAW, SLAVES WERE NOW FREE, BUT THEY WERE STILL NOT EQUAL. MANY WERE VERY POOR.

IN THE SOUTH, AFRICAN AMERICANS HAD TO STAND AT ATTENTION WHEN WHITES PASSED THEM!

IN MOST SOUTHERN STATES, SPECIAL LAWS WERE PASSED. UNDER THESE LAWS, BLACKS COULD NOT OWN CERTAIN KINDS OF PROPERTY! BLACKS COULD NOT OWN GUNS! AND BLACKS COULD NOT VOTE!

VOTE

IN 1896, THE U.S. SUPREME COURT RULED THAT SEPARATION OF RACES, OR SEGREGATION, WAS LEGAL. PUBLIC PLACES WERE SUPPOSED TO BE "SEPARATE BUT EQUAL" FOR BLACKS AND WHITES. BUT THE SCHOOLS FOR BLACK STUDENTS OFTEN DID NOT HAVE BOOKS OR DESKS.

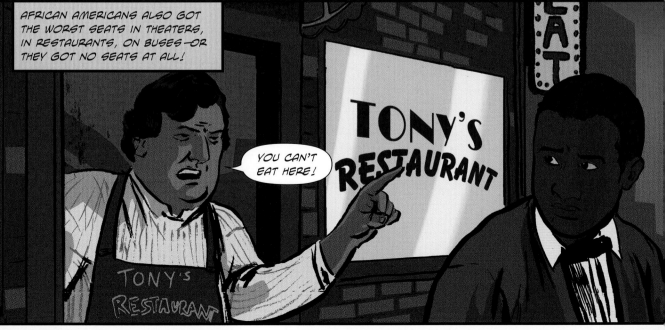

AFRICAN AMERICANS ALSO GOT THE WORST SEATS IN THEATERS, IN RESTAURANTS, ON BUSES—OR THEY GOT NO SEATS AT ALL!

THE NATIONAL ASSOCIATION FOR THE ADVANCEMENT OF COLORED PEOPLE (NAACP) FORMED TO CHANGE THESE UNFAIR LAWS.

EQUAL RIGHTS FOR ALL PEOPLES

DURING THE 1930S, THE NAACP URGED ALL AMERICANS TO STOP THE ABUSE AND MURDER OF BLACK PEOPLE.

A MAN WAS LYNCHED YESTERDAY

EVERY TIME A BLACK PERSON WAS LYNCHED, THIS BANNER WAS HUNG OUTSIDE ITS OFFICES IN NEW YORK CITY. LYNCHING WAS A TERRIFYING FORM OF CRUELTY. IT INVOLVED TORTURING AND KILLING BLACK PEOPLE—USUALLY BY HANGING.

IN 1955, ALABAMA WAS STILL SEGREGATED.
BLACKS HAD TO SIT IN THE BACK OF THE BUS.
IF THE BUS GOT CROWDED, THEY HAD TO GIVE
UP THOSE SEATS TO WHITE PASSENGERS.

HEY!
WAIT!

BLACK PEOPLE HAD TO PAY AT
THE FRONT AND THEN STEP OFF
THE BUS AND REENTER AT THE
BACK. BUS DRIVERS OFTEN
PULLED AWAY, SHOUTING
INSULTS AT THE BLACK PERSON.

STOP!

COLORED TO THE BACK!

ON DECEMBER 1, 1955, IN MONTGOMERY, ROSA PARKS ENTERED A CROWDED BUS AFTER WORK. AS SHE RODE HOME, MORE PEOPLE GOT ON BOARD.

HEY LADY!

THE DRIVER ORDERED ALL BLACK RIDERS TO GIVE UP THEIR SEATS. ROSA PARKS DID NOT WANT TO MOVE!

MOVE OR I'LL CALL THE POLICE!

YOU MAY DO THAT!

SHE WAS ARRESTED AND FORCED TO LEAVE THE BUS.

2857

THE NEWS OF ROSA PARKS'S ARREST SPREAD FAST. MOST BLACK PEOPLE FELT POWERLESS. BUT SOME LEADERS GOT AN IDEA. THE NAACP CONTACTED ROSA PARKS AND ASKED FOR HER HELP.

MRS. PARKS, CAN YOU HELP?

I'LL GO ALONG WITH YOU!

WE'VE GOT TO GET THE WORD OUT!

ANGERED, THE MONTGOMERY BLACK COMMUNITY AND THE NAACP DECIDED TO BOYCOTT THE BUS SYSTEM. IN A BOYCOTT, PEOPLE REFUSE TO BUY GOODS OR USE A SERVICE IN PROTEST AGAINST UNFAIR TREATMENT.

MANY BLACK LEADERS WONDERED IF THE PEOPLE IN MONTGOMERY WOULD HAVE THE COURAGE TO BOYCOTT. THE LOCAL AFRICAN AMERICANS FACED MANY DANGERS. THEY COULD BE FIRED FROM THEIR JOBS. ANGRY WHITES COULD THROW THINGS AT THEM WHILE THEY WALKED INSTEAD OF RODE THE BUS.

NOT ONE AFRICAN AMERICAN BOARDED A MONTGOMERY BUS! BLACK PEOPLE WALKED OR RODE BICYCLES TO WORK. SOME TOOK BLACK-OWNED CABS. THESE CABS OFFERED RIDES FOR THE SAME 10 CENTS THAT THE BUS WOULD HAVE COST. NORMALLY A CAB WOULD COST AT LEAST 45 CENTS.

THANK YOU FOR THE RIDE, SAM. CAN YOU PICK ME UP AT FIVE?

THE NEWLY FORMED MONTGOMERY IMPROVEMENT ASSOCIATION (MIA) CHOSE DR. MARTIN LUTHER KING, JR. TO LEAD THEM. THE MIA GUIDED THE BUS BOYCOTT.

KING FOLLOWED THE TEACHINGS OF MAHATMA GANDHI, A LEADER IN INDIA. GANDHI TAUGHT HIS FOLLOWERS TO FIGHT INJUSTICE WITHOUT USING VIOLENCE. HE URGED THEM TO PROTEST PEACEFULLY BY USING STRIKES AND BOYCOTTS.

EQUAL RIGHTS FOR ALL

EQUALITY

WE DEMA RIGH

RE
R
OL

THIS POLICY OF NONVIOLENCE AND PEACEFUL PROTEST WOULD BE AT THE HEART OF THE CIVIL RIGHTS MOVEMENT. AFTER THE BUS BOYCOTT, MARTIN LUTHER KING, JR. WOULD BECOME KNOWN AS THE LEADER OF THE AFRICAN-AMERICAN CIVIL RIGHTS MOVEMENT.

HE LED MANY NONVIOLENT PROTESTS EVEN IN THE FACE OF HOSTILITY.

THE BLACK COMMUNITY COULD NOT DECIDE HOW LONG TO BOYCOTT.

THE BLACK LEADERS WONDERED HOW LONG BEFORE PEOPLE GREW TIRED OF WALKING.

SOME FEARED RAIN WOULD MAKE THEM WANT TO TAKE THE BUS. SOME FEARED POLICE WOULD FORCE THEM TO TAKE THE BUS.

HEY, YOU BETTER GET BACK ON THE BUS!

WITH KING'S LEADERSHIP, HOWEVER, THE MIA CRUSHED THESE FEARS. HE WAS A SMART, PASSIONATE SPEAKER.
WE ARE HERE THIS EVENING TO SAY TO THOSE WHO HAVE MISTREATED US SO LONG THAT WE ARE TIRED—

—TIRED OF BEING SEGREGATED AND HUMILIATED, TIRED OF BEING KICKED ABOUT BY THE BRUTAL FEET OF OPPRESSION.

MONTGOMERY'S BLACK COMMUNITY AGREED ON THEIR DEMANDS.

DEMAND ONE
Blacks should be treated with respect on buses.

DEMAND TWO
No blacks should be forced to give up their seats. It will be first-come, first-served seating.

DEMAND THREE
Black bus drivers should be hired for routes with black passengers.

MARTIN LUTHER KING, JR. PRESENTED THE MIA'S DEMANDS TO CITY AND BUS COMPANY OFFICIALS.

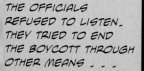

THE OFFICIALS REFUSED TO LISTEN. THEY TRIED TO END THE BOYCOTT THROUGH OTHER MEANS . . .

THEY TRIED TO SCARE THE AFRICAN AMERICANS INTO QUITTING. POLICE ARRESTED AFRICAN AMERICANS FOR BOYCOTTING. POLICE ARRESTED THEM FOR WALKING TO WORK. POLICE ARRESTED WHITE WOMEN FOR DRIVING THEIR BLACK MAIDS TO WORK AND TO HOME. THE CHARGE—SPEEDING.

IT DID NOT SEEM THAT THE MONTGOMERY OFFICIALS WOULD EVER AGREE TO THE THREE DEMANDS. SO A BLACK LAWYER FROM MONTGOMERY FILED A LAWSUIT FOR THE MIA. THE LAWSUIT CHARGED THAT BUS SEGREGATION DID NOT FOLLOW U.S. LAWS.

THE JUDGE LISTENED . . .

. . . AND SEVERAL MONTHS LATER, THE RULING CAME . . .

. . . THE MIA HAD WON!

THE COURT RULED IN FAVOR OF THE MIA, BUT THE CITY OF MONTGOMERY REFUSED TO ACCEPT THE COURT'S DECISION.

MORE TIME PASSED. THE CASE REACHED THE U.S. SUPREME COURT.

ON DECEMBER 20, 1956, THE SUPREME COURT ORDERED THE MONTGOMERY BUSES TO STOP MAKING BLACKS SIT IN THE BACK. ALL RIDERS HAD TO BE TREATED EQUALLY. THE NEXT DAY, KING BOARDED A MONTGOMERY BUS. NATIONAL NEWSPAPERS AND TELEVISION COVERED THE HISTORIC BUS RIDE.

FOR THE NEXT TEN YEARS, BLACKS AND WHITES WORKED TOGETHER TO BRING AN END TO SEGREGATION. THIS WAS THE PEAK TIME OF THE CIVIL RIGHTS MOVEMENT.

BUT CHANGING LAWS AND ATTITUDES WAS SLOW AND DIFFICULT. NOT ALL WHITE PEOPLE ACCEPTED THE CHANGE SO EASILY. BOMBS EXPLODED IN BLACK CHURCHES. A WHITE PERSON SHOT A PREGNANT BLACK WOMAN RIDING A BUS.

MANY PEOPLE LOST THEIR HOMES—AND THEIR LIVES—FIGHTING FOR EQUAL RIGHTS.

FRUSTRATED, BLACK YOUTH DECIDED TO FIGHT BACK WITH SIT-INS. THEY ENTERED RESTAURANTS THAT DID NOT ALLOW BLACKS. THEY WOULD JUST SIT THERE QUIETLY AND REFUSE TO MOVE. USUALLY POLICE OFFICERS WOULD TAKE THEM AWAY AND ARREST THEM. THE ARRESTS GAVE THE STUDENTS MEDIA ATTENTION. THE NEWS MADE MORE PEOPLE AWARE OF THE STUDENTS' WISHES FOR EQUAL TREATMENT FOR EVERYONE.

KING'S SPEECH REACHED THE EARS OF PEOPLE ALL OVER THE COUNTRY. ON JULY 2, 1964, PRESIDENT LYNDON JOHNSON SIGNED THE CIVIL RIGHTS ACT. THIS ACT FORCED PUBLIC PLACES TO PROVIDE EQUAL TREATMENT TO PEOPLE OF ALL COLORS AND RACES. NO LONGER WOULD BLACK PEOPLE HAVE TO SIT IN A DIFFERENT PART OF A THEATER OR RESTAURANT.

UNFORTUNATELY, BLACKS IN THE SOUTH STILL COULD NOT VOTE. THEY HAD NO SAY IN WHO REPRESENTED THEM.

VOTE

THE MONTGOMERY BUS BOYCOTT GAVE THE CIVIL RIGHTS MOVEMENT A NEW, STRONGER VOICE. IT ALSO INSPIRED OTHER GROUPS TO USE PEACEFUL PROTEST TO MAKE THEIR VOICES HEARD.

MARTIN LUTHER KING, JR. HELPED ORGANIZE AND END THE BUS BOYCOTT. HE LED MANY MORE MARCHES AND CHANGED MANY MORE ATTITUDES. TRAGICALLY, HE WAS MURDERED IN 1968. EVERY JANUARY, WE CELEBRATE MARTIN LUTHER KING, JR. DAY TO HONOR HIS POWERFUL ROLE IN THE FIGHT FOR CIVIL RIGHTS.

AND TO HONOR AFRICAN AMERICAN CULTURE AND ALL BLACKS WHO FOUGHT FOR RACIAL EQUALITY, BLACK HISTORY MONTH IS CELEBRATED IN FEBRUARY.

FOR MANY YEARS, ROSA PARKS, THE "MOTHER OF THE CIVIL RIGHTS MOVEMENT," KEPT WORKING FOR EQUAL RIGHTS FOR ALL AMERICANS. IN 1996, SHE RECEIVED THE PRESIDENTIAL MEDAL FOR FREEDOM FROM PRESIDENT CLINTON. IN 1999, SHE WAS AWARDED THE CONGRESSIONAL GOLD MEDAL. ROSA PARKS DIED AT THE AGE OF 92 ON OCTOBER 24, 2005.

TODAY, AFRICAN AMERICANS HAVE MADE MANY GAINS IN AMERICAN SOCIETY. MANY ATTITUDES HAVE CHANGED. BUT BLACK AMERICANS ARE STILL POORER THAN MOST WHITE AMERICANS. THANKS TO THE WORK OF ROSA PARKS, MARTIN LUTHER KING, JR., AND OTHERS LIKE THEM, THEIR VOICES WILL BE HEARD!!

MORE BOOKS TO READ

The Civil Rights Movement for Kids: A History with 21 Activities. Mary Turck (Chicago Review Press)

If a Bus Could Talk: The Story of Rosa Parks. Faith Ringgold (Simon and Schuster Books for Young People).

Martin Luther King Jr. Mary Winget (Lerner Publications)

The Montgomery Bus Boycott. Landmark Events in American History (series). Frank Walsh. (World Almanac Library)

Rosa Parks: My Story. Rosa Parks (Penguin Putnam Books for Young Readers)

WEB SITES

Black American History
www.africanaonline.com/

Heroes & Icons: Rosa Parks
www.time.com/time/time100/heroes/profile/parks01.html

Culture and Change
teacher.scholastic.com/rosa/

Rosa Parks Biography: Academy of Achievement
www.achievement.org/autodoc/page/par0bio-1

Rosa Parks Library and Museum
montgomery.troy.edu/museum/

Please visit our web site at: www.worldalmanaclibrary.com
For a free color catalog describing World Almanac® Library's list of high-quality books and multimedia programs, call 1-800-848-2928 (USA) or 1-800-387-3178 (Canada). World Almanac® Library's fax: (414) 332-3567.

Library of Congress Cataloging-in-Publication Data

O'Hern, Kerri.
    The Montgomery bus boycott / Kerri O'Hern and Frank Walsh.
      p. cm. — (Graphic histories)
    Includes bibliographical references.
    ISBN 0-8368-6205-8 (lib. bdg.)
    ISBN 0-8368-6257-0 (softcover)
    1. Montgomery (Ala.)--Race relations--Juvenile literature. 2. Segregation in transportation—Alabama--Montgomery—History—20th century--Juvenile literature. 3. African Americans—Civil rights—Alabama—Montgomery—History--20th century--Juvenile literature. I. Walsh, Frank. II. Title. III. Series.
F334.M79O38   2006
323.1'196073076147—dc22
                        2005027874

First published in 2006 by
World Almanac® Library
A Member of the WRC Media Family of Companies
330 West Olive Street, Suite 100
Milwaukee, WI 53212 USA

Copyright © 2006 by World Almanac® Library.

Produced by Design Press, a division of the
Savannah College of Art and Design
Design: Janice Shay and Maria Angela Rojas
Editing: Kerri O'Hern
Illustration: D. McHargue
World Almanac® Library editorial direction: Mark Sachner and Valerie J. Weber
World Almanac® Library art direction: Tammy West

Printed in the United States of America